15

AMAZING & INSPIRING
TRUE TALES

FROM BASKETBALL'S GREATEST
GUARDS OF ALL TIME

TERRENCE ARMSTRONG

CONTENTS

INTRODUCTION

Basketball was invented by Dr. James Naismith, a Canadian teacher of physical education, in the late 1800s. Back then, the sport didn't even have an official name, and it was played with a soccer ball! But it quickly gained popularity, becoming a US sport within 10 years. A professional league was formed in 1898, and basketball was included in the Olympics for the first time in 1936.

The game is fast-paced, high-energy, and a lot of fun to both play and watch. Since its inception, it has been played in school playgrounds, at home, and on professional courts around the globe. Over the years, there have been some truly great players who have left their mark on the game and in the hearts of fans. Point guards, in particular, are a crowd favorite. The position requires a fast and mobile playing style, and results in a lot of long-distance shooting opportunities and dramatic baskets. Many of the greatest players of all time were guards—and for good reason!

In this book, we're going to take a look at the stories of some of the greatest guards of all time. They may just inspire you to become the next basketball legend!

MAGIC JOHNSON
THE SHOWTIME MAESTRO

Earvin "Magic" Johnson, Jr. was born in Lansing, Michigan, where his father, Earvin Johnson Sr., worked on the assembly line at General Motors. Meanwhile, his mother was the school janitor.

Magic Johnson was part of a large family. His father had three children from a previous marriage, and Johnson had six directly related siblings. His father and mother worked extremely hard. In fact, Johnson often joined his father at his evening job, collecting garbage. This led to other kids calling him "Garbage Man."

Johnson fell in love with basketball while he was growing up. It was a sport he could play anywhere—and that's exactly what he did! At the time, his idols were Bill Russell, Earl Monroe, and Marques Haynes. To help Johnson fully understand basketball, his father (who played in high school), taught him the finer points of the game.

By the time he was 13, Johnson was the dominant player at his junior high school, and he was starting to think about a future as a professional. But first, he was excited about heading to high school! The local school, Sexton, had a very successful basketball team. Unfortunately, he ended up going to Everett High School, instead. This meant riding the bus every day and attending a predominantly white school, where racism was a major problem. People would throw stones at the bus the Black students rode on, and none of the White basketball players would talk to Johnson.

It took some time, but Johnson eventually accepted the situation for what it was. It allowed him to play basketball, and he seized every opportunity he could. At 15 years of age, he logged his first triple-double of 36 points, 18 rebounds, and 16 assists. He was a sophomore at the time, and his performance earned him the nickname "Magic," which stuck with him throughout his career.

In his final year at Everett, Johnson led the team, establishing a 27-1 win-loss record and winning the state championship. By the time he finished high school, he had two All-State selections and was being called the best high school player Michigan had ever produced.

For college, Johnson decided he wanted to stay close to home. He accepted an invitation to join Michigan State, because the coach said he would be allowed to play as a point guard. The college also already had some great talent, which made it easier for Johnson to say yes.

Johnson was the team's top scorer during his freshman year. Then, during the 1978-79 season, he led Michigan State to a 75-64 defeat of Indiana State, winning the NCAA tournament and being named most outstanding player of the Final Four. At the time, this was the most-watched college basketball game ever.

Unsurprisingly, Johnson was selected first overall in the 1979 NBA Draft. The Lakers signed him and gave him the point guard position. One of his best performances ever came the following year, in the 1980 NBA Finals. The Lakers managed to secure a 3-2 lead in the series, but then their center, Kareem Abdul-Jabbar, sprained his ankle, leaving him unable to play. Johnson had to pay the sixth game starting as the team's center—a position he was unaccustomed to playing. During the game, he ended up playing in the guard, center, and forward positions, logging 42 points, 15 rebounds, seven assists, and three steals. The Lakers won the game 123-107, and in doing so won the NBA championship. Johnson's performance in the game is regarded as one of the finest in the history of the sport, and he became one of just four players to have won the NCAA and NBA championships in consecutive years.

The following year was not so kind to Johnson. He tore the cartilage in his knee and was forced to sit out most of the season. He admits to being depressed during this time, although a new contract (the highest-value sports contract in history, at that point) helped him see the way forward.

Johnson continued to play with the Lakers. In fact, he stayed with them for the remainder of his extremely successful career. Much of his success came because he was such a versatile player. In addition to his shooting skills, he is considered one of the best passers the NBA has ever seen. This was evident in 1984, when he played against the Phoenix Suns and completed a record 24 assists in one game.

Of course, Johnson was a prolific scorer, as well. Perhaps one of his greatest accomplishments was during the 1987 season, when he played 80 games for the Lakers and scored an average of 23.9 points per game. The Lakers won 65 games that year.

The 1987 NBA finals also showcased his amazing talent. The Lakers were already leading the series, 2-1. In the fourth game, Boston was ahead with just seven seconds left, but Johnson nailed a skyhook over Kevin McHale and clinched the game for the Lakers, who once again went on to win the championship.

While Johnson's career was full of fantastic individual plays, he was a great team player and helped the Lakers win back-to-back NBA championships in 1987 and 1988. They were the first team to have done so since Bill Russell's Celtics in 1956 and 1957. Johnson was instrumental to this achievement, and was also part of the "Dream Team" that won gold at the 1992 Summer Olympics, capping off an already illustrious career!

FUN FACTS ABOUT MAGIC JOHNSON

1. Johnson is an impressive 6 feet 9 inches tall!
2. He briefly coached the Lakers at the end of the 1994 season.
3. His entire professional career was spent with the Lakers.
4. Johnson averaged 11.2 assists per game during his career, which is the highest average in NBA history.
5. He was inducted into the Hall of Fame in 2002.

QUICK TRIVIA TEST

1. What was Magic Johnson's birth name?

Earvin Johnson Jr.

2. What did the other children call him when he was young?

Garbage Man.

3. Who were his idols when he was growing up?

Bill Russell, Earl Monroe, and Marques Haynes.

4. How did he get the name Magic Johnson?

As a sophomore, he earned a triple-double of 36 points, 18 rebounds, and 16 assists.

5. In which year was he drafted by the Lakers?

1979.

FIVE LIFE LESSONS

1. Get outside your comfort zone.

Johnson once said, "As I look back on it today, I see the whole picture very differently. It's true that I hated missing out on Sexton. And the first few months, I was miserable at Everett. But being bused to Everett turned out to be one of the best things that ever happened to me. It got me out of my own little world and taught me how to understand White people, how to communicate and deal with them." Hindsight is a wonderful thing, and illustrates how beneficial it can be to get outside your comfort zone.

2. Never quit.

All athletes have ups and downs in their careers, and despite his many successes, Johnson was no different. However, he never quit. In fact, he once said, "There's winning and there's losing, and in life, both will happen. What is never acceptable to me is quitting."

3. Reach for your dreams.

Magic Johnson always had talent. He also had a dream to become a professional basketball player. It was that dream that encouraged him to work hard and succeed. You should choose a dream and go for it. As Johnson once said, "You're the only one who can make the difference. Whatever your dream, go for it."

4. It takes more than talent to succeed—hard work is also essential.

Johnson once said, "Talent is never enough. With few exceptions, the best players are the hardest workers." It's worth remembering that working hard toward your goal will help you succeed.

5. Teamwork matters.

Johnson played on a team and learned to be a great team player. That, along with his talent, drove the Lakers success. It's important to remember that teamwork makes a real difference. You need to learn to work with others, and it's never too early to start practicing that.

MICHAEL JORDAN
THE GREATEST OF ALL TIME

Michael Jeffrey Jordan was born in February 1963 in Brooklyn, New York City. Although no one could have known it at the time, he would go on to be the most famous basketball player in the world. When Jordan was born, his parents already had three other children. And a fifth arrived after Jordan, giving him a house full of siblings to play with!

Jordan loved sports from a young age. After moving to Wilmington, North Carolina, he attended Emsley A. Laney High School, where he played basketball, baseball, and football. He was a natural athlete, and sports came easily to him. Ironically, when he first tried out for the varsity basketball team, he was just 5 feet 11 inches tall, and didn't make the team because they thought he was too short!

In retrospect, this rejection was a good thing. It gave Jordan the additional motivation he needed to prove his value. He worked hard and became the star of the junior varsity team. The following year, thanks to a growth spurt and some serious training, Jordan earned his spot on the varsity team. Over the next two seasons, he averaged more 25 points per game. This culminated in an appearance in the 1981 McDonalds All-American Game, where he scored 30 points and was quickly approached by recruiters from numerous colleges.

Jordan accepted a scholarship to the University of North Carolina, where he studied cultural geography. Although he was drafted into the NBA during his junior year, he eventually returned to the school to complete his undergraduate degree!

In 1984, Jordan was the third overall pick in the NBA Draft, and ended up signing with the Chicago Bulls. The only reason he was the third pick was because the first two teams needed centers, and Jordan was a shooting guard.

While playing for the Bulls between 1984 and 1993, Jordan was voted the NBA Most Valuable Player three times. He also helped the Bulls win the NBA championship in 1991, 1992, and 1993. In addition to these championships, one of the most memorable moments from this era was in 1985, when Jordan was playing a Nike exhibition game in Trieste, Italy. During the game, he dunked the ball so hard that he smashed the glass on the backboard!

Jordan retired in 1993 to play Minor League baseball, but soon returned to play for the Bulls from 1995 through 1999. This second part of his basketball career was full of highlights, including the 1998 NBA championship against the Utah Jazz. With 5.2 seconds remaining in the fourth quarter, Jordan snuck a beautiful cross-over past Jazz forward Bryan Russell and hit a jump shot from behind the free throw line. He put the Bulls up 87-86, winning them the game and the championship.

Jordan retired again in 1999, but once again this retirement only lasted two years. During that time, he became part owner of the Washington Wizards. Then, in 2001, he announced that he would be playing for the Wizards. He finally retired from basketball for good in 2003, leaving behind one of the greatest legacies in the sport. He won six NBA championships, six NBA finals MPVs, and 5 NBA MVPs, received 14 NBA All-Star selections, and set a host of records that may never be broken. Since his retirement, he has been committed to giving back to the sport.

Of course, Jordan's excellence on the court wasn't limited to his career in the NBA. He also played for the US national team on several occasions. His first appearance was at the 1983 Pan American Games, when he helped the US win a gold medal. He then won gold in the 1984 Summer Olympics, and was an integral part of the 1992 Dream Team, which won the 1992 Tournament of Americas and the 1992 Summer Olympics. In short, when Jordan played, the US team won virtually every major tournament it entered—a fitting tribute to the greatest player of all time.

FUN FACTS ABOUT
MICHAEL JORDAN

1. Jordan was the leading scorer in the NBA for 10 consecutive seasons.
2. He is known for sticking out his tongue as he dunks, a trait he gets from his father.
3. Jordan was in the 1996 film "Space Jam," where he played himself.
4. He always ate a 23-ounce New York steak, mashed potatoes, and a salad four hours before a game.
5. One pair of Air Jordans worn by Jordan sold for $71,000 at auction!

QUICK TRIVIA TEST

1. What is Michael Jordan's full name?

Michael Jeffrey Jordan.

2. How many brothers and sisters does he have?

Four.

3. Why didn't he make his high school varsity team?

He was considered to be too short.

4. Why was he frozen out in his rookie season?

Veterans were upset he was receiving too much attention.

5. What year was his first retirement?

1993.

FIVE LIFE LESSONS

1. You can find motivation anywhere.

Jordan was turned down by his high school's varsity team during a year when only one sophomore made the team. He could simply have accepted this rejection, but instead he saw it as a chance to prove himself. You never know what opportunities you'll be handed or what will motivate you. Be open to anything!

2. Have a backup plan.

It may seem strange, but, even if you're dedicated to becoming a professional sports player, it is important to have a backup plan. Jordan studied cultural geography in college, which gave him career options. After all, no matter how talented he was, you never know when an injury might strike.

3. Adversity can come at any time.

You would think that Jordan's teammates would have appreciated his skills, but instead they froze him out during his rookie year. That could have been disheartening and affected Jordan's performance, but instead he just worked harder to prove his worth, giving his teammates no excuse to freeze him out.

4. Follow your heart.

The world was shocked when Jordan announced his retirement in 1993. But, for various reasons, he needed a break. He followed his heart, and when he came back to the game, he continued being the best player in the world. That may not have happened if he hadn't taken some time off.

5. It's okay to fail.

Jordan has an impressive record, but even he didn't win or succeed every time. As he said, "I can accept failure—everyone fails at something. But I can't accept not trying." It's okay to fail, as long as you always try.

LARRY BIRD
THE LEGENDARY RIVAL
OF MAGIC JOHNSON

Larry Joe Bird was born on December 7, 1956, in West Baden Springs, Indiana. He had four brothers and one sister, and his family had a mixed heritage, with traces of Irish, Scottish, and Native American.

Bird grew up poor. His father struggled after serving in the Korean War and his mother worked two jobs to support them all. Sadly, his parents divorced when Bird was in high school, and a year later his troubled dad committed suicide. Bird states that his struggles as a kid inspired him to play basketball and motivated him to be the best he could be. He maintained that motivation throughout his career.

Basketball was Bird's escape. He started playing as a youngster, on the courts near his home. He then played for Springs Valley High School, where he averaged 31 points, 21 rebounds, and four assists per game. He ultimately became the school's all-time top scorer. During these formative years, he idolized Mel Daniels, the 6 foot 9-inch center for the Indiana Pacers.

Bird's motivation, practice, and talent paid off, as he received a scholarship to study and play college ball for the Indiana Hoosiers. Unfortunately, the change from small-town schooling to big-city campus life was too much for the young Bird. After just one month, he dropped out and enrolled at Northwood Institute instead.

After working multiple jobs for a year, Bird enrolled at Indiana State University in 1975. He played ball for the university team and helped them reach the NCAA tournament championship. Unfortunately, they lost the final game—but Bird had put himself on the map. The game had the highest-ever television rating for a college basketball game because Bird and Magic Johnson were playing against each other.

It was obvious that Bird would play professionally, and he was the sixth overall pick in the 1978 NBA draft. He finished the season with Indiana State, then started with the Boston Celtics in 1979. Interestingly, there was a protracted fight over money before he started. At the time, the Celtics' general manager stated he wouldn't pay Bird more than any of the other current players, but Bird's agent stated that they would reject any offer they didn't find satisfactory and enter the 1979 draft instead. Bird won the negotiation and received a $3.25 million contract, becoming the highest paid rookie in history.

It was money well spent. In his first season, Bird helped the Celtics become a legitimate contender. In his first NBA game, he scored 14 points, and by the end of the season he had averaged 21.3 points per game.

Things got even better in 1980 when the Celtics signed Kevin McHale and Robert Parish. They teamed up with Bird to create a Hall of Fame trio, and the three players are still regarded as one of the finest front courts any NBA team has ever had! That year, the Celtics won the NBA championship.

Despite an impressive series of performances, the following season saw the Celtics lose the title in the final, and the year after that they lost in the conference semifinals. Things swung back in their favor in 1983, however, when they defeated Magic Johnson and the Lakers in the NBA finals. Bird also won his first finals MVP award.

One of the highlights of Bird's career came in March of the 1984-1985 season, when he scored 60 points against the Atlanta Hawks. Unfortunately, while the team made it to the finals against the Lakers that year, they weren't able to pull off the win and during the offseason, Bird hurt his back shoveling rock for his mom, which led to back problems for the rest of his career.

That didn't stop the biggest rivalry in the NBA from continuing. Bird and the Celtics were constantly battling Magic and the Lakers. Every time the two teams met, there was a huge audience. It helped that the two teams' main stars were complete opposites. Magic was black, Bird was white. Magic was a showman, while Bird was more of an introvert. The Lakers focused on offense and putting on a good show, whereas the Celtics focused on defense and were very physical. However, in a fantastic example of how a sports rivalry doesn't have to extend off the court, Bird and Magic actually became close friends. Magic even appeared at Bird's retirement ceremony, where he said that they were "friends forever."

After incredible performances in the 1987-88 season, Bird began to suffer a number of injuries that impacted his ability to play. The 1988-89 season was cut short for Bird, as he had bone spurs surgically removed from his heels. The following season saw him deal with serious back issues, which ultimately led to his retirement. Yet, despite the injuries, in his final three seasons with the Celtics, he averaged 20 points per game and was still considered one of the premier players in the league.

After retiring, Bird continued to have an outside influence on the game of basketball. He served as the Celtics special assistant for a time before transferring to the Indiana Pacers as a coach, where he led them to a 58-24 record, the best they had ever done.

FUN FACTS ABOUT LARRY BIRD

1. Bird is the only person in the NBA to win MVP, coach of the year, and executive of the year.
2. He was famous for telling his opponents when and where he would score.
3. He played for the Celtics for his entire professional career.
4. Bird appeared in the 1996 film "Space Jam"
5. despite having serious back problems, Bird was part of the 1992 Dream Team.

QUICK TRIVIA TEST

1. When was Bird born?

December 7, 1956.

2. How many brothers does he have?

Four. He also has one sister.

3. What pick was he in the 1978 NBA draft?

Sixth overall.

4. How did Bird hurt his back?

Shoveling crushed rock for his mom's driveway.

5. Which team did the Celtics have a strong rivalry with?

The Los Angeles Lakers.

FIVE LIFE LESSONS

1. Always try to be the best.

The only player potentially better than Bird in his time was Magic Johnson. The two had an intense rivalry, yet they were also the best of friends. Their constant efforts to be better than each other made for great televised sports and ensured they were both playing at the peak of their abilities.

2. Confidence counts.

Bird was known for announcing when he would score, and even where! That's a lot of confidence going into a game, but more often than not he'd do exactly what he'd predicted. Being confident certainly helped him achieve great things, and it can help you, too.

3. Work hard.

Bird once said, "A winner is someone who recognizes his God-given talents, works his tail off to develop them into skills, and uses these skills to accomplish his goals." In short, no matter how great your talent is, you have to work hard if you want to succeed.

4. Do what you do best.

It can often seem hard to follow a dream and do what you feel most passionate about. However, as difficult as it may seem, you should focus on what you do best and find a way to keep doing it. As Bird said, "The best players will play." You just have to find a way.

5. Don't let success go to your head.

Winning is a great feeling, regardless of what you're doing. However, winning is only one moment, and then you need to focus on the next. As Bird said, "Don't let winning make you soft. Don't let losing make you quit. Don't let your teammates down in any situation." Enjoy your success, but remember that it's temporary unless you keep trying.

OSCAR ROBERTSON
THE BIG O'S TRIPLE-DOUBLE LEGACY

Oscar Palmer Robertson was born on November 24, 1938, in Charlotte, Tennessee. Like many people during the Great Depression, his family was extremely poor. When Robertson was 18 months old, his family moved to Indianapolis, Indiana, in search of work and a better life. They moved into a segregated housing project. At the time, separating White and Black people was commonplace. In fact, it wasn't until 1948 that President Truman signed an executive order ending segregation in the military, and segregation in the US didn't officially end until 1964.

As a poor kid struggling with racism Robertson turned to basketball for comfort. He learned how to shoot the ball with tennis balls, and even rags wrapped in elastic bands. A peach basket at the back of his house served as a net.

While Robertson showed some signs of talent early on, it was his high school coach, Ray Crowe, who steered him in the right direction. Crowe was focused on creating a fundamentally sound game. That meant Robertson had to understand and be able to play all the positions. He earned a place on the Crispus Attucks High School team under Crowe, and started playing for them as a sophomore, when they made it all the way to the state semifinals. This season later became the basis of the movie "Hoosiers."

His junior year was a different story. Robertson led the Attucks in dominating their opponents. They won the state championship in 1955, becoming the first Indianapolis team to win a championship in the Hoosier tournament. They also won the following season, becoming the first team in Indiana to win back-to-back championships.

Roberston played for the Cincinnati Bearcats in college. During his time there, he logged an impressive average of 33.8 points per game. Each year he was at college, he won the national scoring title and was chosen as College Player of the Year. He set 14 NCAA records and another 19 school records, many of which still stand today. For example, his record of 62 points in one game has not yet been broken. He also had six games with over 50 points and 10 college triple-doubles, none of which have been matched.

After finishing college in 1960, Robertson was nominated to be co-captain of the US basketball team. The team was considered the greatest assembly of basketball talent the world had ever seen. Unsurprisingly, they flattened the opposition and won gold at the 1960 Olympics. Robertson started as a forward, but was also able to play point guard when needed. A total of 10 of the players on the team went on to play in the NBA, three of whom later joined Robertson in the Hall of Fame.

Robertson was picked by the Cincinnati Royals in the 1960 NBA Draft. In his debut game, he earned 21 points and helped the Royals beat the Lakers 140-123. In his rookie season, he averaged 30.5 points per game, giving him the title of Rookie of the Season.

During the 1961-62 season, Robertson was the first player in the history of the NBA to average a triple-double for the whole year. He also set the record for the most triple-doubles in a season, with 41—a record that stood until 2016. He also logged 899 assists, significantly more than the previous record of 715, set by Bob Cousy. His team also made it to the 1962 NBA playoffs, although they ended up losing early.

The following season, Robertson averaged 28.3 points per game and almost logged another triple-double season. His team made it to the Eastern Division finals, but failed to win. Impressively, Robertson also managed to average a triple-double over his first five seasons in the NBA with the Cincinnati Royals!

Although his performance continued to be impressive, the Royals struggled during the 1964/1965 season. In fact, they didn't make it past the first round of the playoffs between 1965 and 1967. Then, they failed to make the playoffs altogether in 1968 and 1969.

A surprise trade in 1970 saw Robertson move to the Bucks. This ended up being a great transition for Robertson. He went from a lackluster team to playing alongside a rising star—Lew Alcindor, better known as Kareem Abdul-Jabbar. The two players fit together perfectly, and the Bucks logged a league-best record of 66-16, which included a 20-game winning streak. They went on to dominate the 1971 NBA playoffs and took the NBA title. Robertson scored 22 points in the final game, but more importantly, he finally got his NBA championship win.

While his achievements on the court were impressive, one of Robertson's most important contributions happened off the court. He was central to an antitrust lawsuit filed by the NBA's Player Association against the NBA. Since he was president of the Players Association, the case became known as Robertson V. National Basketball Association. The lawsuit sought to block the merging of the American Basketball Association (ABA) with the National Basketball Association (NBA). The lawsuit also wanted to end the clause that bound a player to a single NBA team, as well as end the NBA's college draft rule binding a player to one team. It also sought to end restrictions on free-agent signings and obtain damages for NBA players financially harmed by these restrictions.

The lawsuit stopped the NBA and ABA from merging in 1970. It wasn't settled until 1976, when the NBA finally agreed to let players become free agents, provided their old team had a right of first refusal allowing them to match any offer received. This meant that players could now talk to other clubs before their contracts expired. The increase in free agents also managed to increase salaries for NBA players—a significant achievement for a player who had grown up in poverty!

FUN FACTS ABOUT OSCAR ROBERTSON

1. He is one of very few NBA players to achieve a triple-double season average.
2. He is a successful author.
3. Robertson won an Olympic Gold in 1960.
4. In 1980, he was inducted into the Naismith Memorial Basketball Hall of Fame.
5. In 2018, he received the NBA Lifetime Achievement Award.

QUICK TRIVIA TEST

1. When was Robertson born?

1938.

2. In which year did he win gold at the Olympics?

1960.

3. In which year did he finally win the NBA championship?

1971.

4. In which year did he win the state championship?

1955.

5. What court case did he eventually win?

Robertson V. National Basketball Association.

FIVE LIFE LESSONS

1. You never know when your luck will change.

Robertson was struggling with the Royals. A lack of high-caliber teammates meant he was consistently bogged down, despite his obvious skill. As disagreements with the team's management grew, he was eventually transferred. It turned out to be a great opportunity for him, giving him his first NBA championship title.

2. Don't settle for less than you deserve.

Robertson was a legend on the court, regularly setting records and leading his team to victory. However, despite his success, he could see the issues within the system and took steps to address them. His iconic lawsuit was a big step in the right direction for all players.

3. Always start with the basics.

It doesn't matter what you're trying to learn, you need to master the basic moves first. Robertson's first coach gave him a fundamental understanding of the game, which transformed his natural ability into legitimate skill on the court.

4. Change is important if you want to succeed.

Robertson once said, "When you play against different people from all walks of life, you can't do the same thing against every player defensively or offensively. You have to change up the way you go at a player." In other words, flexibility and the ability to change is essential to winning.

5. There is always room for improvement.

Robertson once said, "When I started playing, I wasn't fast, I was gangly, my jump shot was terrible." Today, he is seen as one of the best athletes to ever play the game. That's because he practiced and improved.

I have included these free downloadable gifts to help light up your inner inspiration & reach your potential.

While you are reading through the stories, lessons and trivia, we recommend that you make use of all the bonuses we've attached here!

All our bonuses have been made specifically to help young athletes feel fired up, get inspired from the best to ever do it, and most importantly fall more in love with this incredible game!

Here's a list of what you're getting:

1) 250 Fun Facts From The World Of Sports
2) Sports Practice and Game Calendar
3) 5 Fun Exercise Drills for Kids
4) The BEST Advice From The Greatest Athletes Of All Time
5) The Mental Mindset Guided Meditation & Affirmation Collection
6) The Most Famous Events In Sports History And What They Can Teach Us

Now, it's over to you to scan the QR code, follow the instructions & get started!

JERRY WEST
THE LOGO'S ICONIC CAREER

Jerry Alan West was born on 28 May, 1938, in Chelyan, West Virginia. His parents already had four children, making him the fifth—and a sixth would soon arrive! Unfortunately, West wasn't born into a happy household. When he was young, his father physically abused him. West has even said that for a while he slept with a loaded shotgun under his bed. He feared having to use it but felt it was the only line of defense available to him.

Despite this, West was an outgoing child. Unfortunately, his older brother was killed during the Korean War, and the loss changed, Jerry, who became introverted and shy overnight. As a youngster, he was also weak. His doctor gave him regular vitamin injections and made him avoid sports, as he feared West would be injured easily. As a result, he spent much of his childhood fishing. But he also spent a lot of time shooting basketballs. His neighbor had secured a basket to his shed, allowing West to practice shooting without actually playing basketball and risking injury. He did it for fun, but he soon developed an uncanny ability to sink baskets from just about anywhere on the court.

When he got older, West went to East Bank High School. He wasn't allowed to play basketball during his freshman year, as he was too short. However, his coach, Duke Shaver, emphasized how important conditioning and defense were. West took this to heart and started working on his stamina and defensive abilities.

Thanks to a growth spurt over the summer, West was eventually allowed to join the team, and ultimately became the starting small forward. He quickly showed everyone how good he was, and was soon recognized as one of the finest West Virginia high school players of his generation.

During this period, West developed his famous mid-range jump shot. It became his go-to shot when he was under pressure from the opposing defense, and was an efficient way for him to score. He led the school to the state championship in 1956, which was a big moment in the school's history. From that year until the school closed in 1999, it changed its name from East Bank to West Bank in celebration of West every year on the date of that incredible game.

After West graduated, he had over 60 universities interested in him. After careful consideration, he chose to stay in West Virginia. He joined the university's basketball team and helped it log a perfect record—17 games without a loss in one season. The following year, he started in all of the team's games and won a variety of awards, including Most Valuable Player.

With an average of 26.6 points per game and a collection of honors, including being named a member of the US Pan American Games basketball team, West quickly became a household name. He also became known for his toughness in the face of adversity. For example, when playing for West Virginia University against the Kentucky Wildcats, he broke his nose. Instead of quitting, he continued to play. For the second half of the game, he played through the pain, even though he was only able to breathe through his mouth. He managed to score 19 points, helping West Virginia win.

Unsurprisingly, West was the second overall pick in the 1960 NBA Draft. He was signed by the Minneapolis Lakers, who shortly afterward moved to Los Angeles. His college coach was hired at the same time, and continued to coach West with the Lakers.

At first, West struggled to settle in. His accent and high-pitched voice made him an easy target for his teammates. But his defensive abilities and ability to jump 16 inches higher than the rim of the basket quickly impressed them. He was also dedicated, spending hours trying to improve his game after everyone else had finished practicing.

With West onboard, the Lakers went from 25 wins the previous season to 36 wins with him. He quickly gained a reputation for late-game shots, and was often referred to as "Mr. Clutch."

West continued to maintain his form, and during the 1964-65 season he averaged an impressive 31 points per game. In the first round of the playoffs that year, the team captain, Baylor, suffered a serious knee injury. The team was shocked, but West took over the captaincy for the remainder of the game and, seemingly by willpower alone, led the Lakers to victory. Sadly, the short-handed Lakers didn't go on to make it to the championships.

With West leading the team, the Lakers finally won the 1972 NBA finals against the Celtics. After six games, the two teams were tied. Game 7 was held in Boston, giving Celtics the home court advantage. The Lakers trailed for most of the game, but toward the end, West hit several clutch baskets, tying the game. Jones tipped the final basket in during overtime to give the Lakers the win and start one of the greatest rivalries in NBA history.

West continued to have an incredible career, becoming only the third player in NBA history to reach 25,000 points. However, statistics only tell so much of the story. It was his ability to seemingly pull a basket out thin air that made him one of the greatest players of all time. A great example was when he made a 60-foot swish in the dying seconds of the 1970 NBA Finals against the New York Knicks, tying the game and sending it to overtime.

Although West only won a single NBA championship, he took his team to the finals an incredible nine times during his 14-season career. It's hard to argue with results like that!

FUN FACTS ABOUT JERRY WEST

1. West was an All-Star every year of his professional career.
2. He played for the Lakers for 14 years.
3. West broke his nose at least nine times playing professional basketball.
4. In the 1961-62 season, he averaged 30.8 points per game. He then kept the average above 30 for the next four seasons!
5. After he retired and left the Lakers, he spent five years as the president of basketball operations for the Memphis Grizzlies.

QUICK TRIVIA TEST

1. What is West's full name?

Jerry Alan West.

2. How many brothers and sisters does West have?

Five.

3. What did his high school do in honor of him?

Changed its name from East Bank to West Bank one day every year.

4. What year did he win his first NBA championship?

1972.

5. How many seasons did he play for the Lakers?

14.

FIVE LIFE LESSONS

1. Don't let physical challenges hold you back.

West is considered one of the best basketball players the sport has ever seen. However, as a child, he was small and extremely frail. His doctor even told him he couldn't play sports. Despite this, West managed to become a professional basketball player, showing that you should never let physical challenges hold you back.

2. Listen to others.

West learned his first lesson about basketball before he was even allowed to join the team. His high school coach illustrated the importance of conditioning and defense, and West took this advice to heart. It helped shape him as a player.

3. Remember you're part of a team.

West was a great player, frequently pulling victories out of seemingly nowhere. However, after the Lakers won the 1972 NBA Finals, West said, "I played terrible basketball in the Finals, and we won... It was particularly frustrating because I was playing so poorly that the team overcame me. Maybe that's what a team is all about." It may have taken him a while to realize it, but the rest of the team was just as important as him.

4. Keep trying, even when you don't feel like it.

West was known for his commitment to training, even when he didn't feel like it. As he once said, "You can't get much done in life if you only work on the days when you feel good." If you want to succeed, you need to keep trying and doing, regardless of how you feel.

5. Set high goals.

West was known as a perfectionist, and was often surprised when he missed shots. You don't need to be a perfectionist to succeed, but you do need to set goals for yourself. It's a good idea to set the bar high, as it will make you reach higher and try harder—and you may even be surprised at the results. As West says, "You need lofty goals."

KOBE BRYANT
THE MAMBA MENTALITY AND
SPORTING EXCELLENCE

Kobe Bean Bryant was born on August 23, 1978, in Philadelphia. He's the youngest of three siblings, but the only son of Pamela Cox Bryant and Joe Bryant. Interestingly, his father, Joe Bryant, was also an NBA player, as was his maternal uncle, John "Chubby" Cox.

Kobe started playing basketball at just three years of age—not surprising, considering his family. As a child, his favorite team was the Lakers. When Kobe was six years old, his father retired from the NBA and the family moved to Italy, where his dad continued playing professional basketball. Young Kobe quickly learned and became fluent in Italian. He also started to get serious about basketball. His grandfather, still in the US, regularly sent tapes of games for him to study.

Between 1987 and 1989, Kobe worked as a ball and mop boy for Olimpia Basket Pistoia, where his father played. He used the job as an opportunity to practice—whenever the team took a half-time break, he'd been on the court practicing. Kobe would also return to the US every summer, allowing him to play and improve in the basketball summer league.

When Kobe was 13, his family moved back to the US for good. His skills started to show as soon as he started playing at Lower Merion High School. He was the first freshman in decades to make the varsity team, and in his third year, he was named

Pennsylvania Player of the Year. His teammate, Kevin Garnett, was selected in the 1995 NBA Draft, skipping college, which made Bryant think about doing the same. Ultimately, despite the fact that his basketball skills and SAT score of 1080 gave him access to virtually any college, he chose to go straight to the NBA. He was only the sixth player to ever do so.

In 1996, after a slightly confusing draft where Bryant was originally selected by the Hornets but then instantly traded to the Lakers, he officially became a Lakers player. He would spend the next 20 years playing for his childhood favorite team!

Kobe's first game was in the Summer Pro League in Long Beach, California, where he scored 25 points in front of a standing-room-only crowd. It was immediately clear that defenders were struggling to get in front of him. Later, in the final, he scored an impressive 36 points, despite being the youngest player in the league, the second-youngest player ever to play in an NBA game, and the youngest NBA starter ever.

During his first season, Kobe averaged just 15.5 minutes of playing time per game. Still, he made his mark. He took part in the Rookie Challenge and won the 1997 Slam Dunk Contest, making him the youngest dunk champion ever.

His second season saw his play time increase, but it was during his third season, in 1998-99, when Kobe became the premier guard on the Lakers, and arguably in the entire league. At the end of this season, he upgraded his three-year, $3.25 million contract for a six-year, $70 million contract! At this stage, he was being compared to Magic Johnson and Michael Jordan. However, it wasn't until the Lakers changed coaches in 1999 that Bryant and his teammates finally reached their full potential. The Lakers won the 2000, 2001, and 2002 NBA championships!

Kobe continued to play for the Lakers until 2016, spending all 20 years with the team and becoming the first NBA guard to play 20 seasons. He won five NBA championships, two NBA Finals MVP awards, four NBA All-Star MVP awards, and made the All-Star team 18 out of his 20 seasons. Kobe was the all-time scoring leader for the Lakers, and is widely considered to have been one of the greatest NBA players of all time. He also gave himself the nickname the "Black Mamba," which became popular with his millions of fans.

Despite all of his talent and success, Kobe only began playing for the US national team in 2007. Due to a series of unfortunate events, he was selected several times but was unable to play. His first shot was on the 2007 USA Men's Senior National Team, which finished 10-0 to win gold in the USA's FIBA Americas Championship Games. Kobe started in all 10 games and averaged 15.3 points per game. He also played for the USA in the 2008 Summer Olympics, helping the team to win gold with an average of 15 points per game. He repeated this feat with the US team in 2012, helping them to win another gold before finishing his national career. Ultimately, he won gold in every tournament he contested, and ended his US national team career with a 26-0 record!

Sadly, Kobe and his daughter died in a tragic accident in 2020. The entire basketball world mourned the loss of one of the greatest to ever play the game.

FUN FACTS ABOUT KOBE BRYANT

1. Kobe started playing basketball when he was three years old!
2. A statue is being built outside the Crypto.com Arena commemorating the 20 seasons he played with the Lakers.
3. Kobe holds the record for the most points ever scored by a Los Angeles Laker.
4. He once scored 81 points in an NBA game—only Wilt Chamberlain has done better.
5. Kobe was the youngest basketball player to score 26,000 points.

QUICK TRIVIA TEST

1. What was Kobe's full name?

Kobe Bean Bryant.

2. Where did he work between 1987-1989?

Olimpia Basket Pistoia, as a ball and mop boy.

3. Which year was he drafted by the Lakers?

1996.

4. Which season did he become the premier guard in the league?

1998-99.

5. Which year did he win his first gold medal with the US team?

2007.

FIVE LIFE LESSONS

1. Use your situation to improve yourself.

Bryant had a near-perfect career, but he still recognized that there are always opportunities to do better. As he once said, "Everything negative—pressure, challenges—is all an opportunity for me to rise." Apply the same thinking to everything you do in life.

2. Hard work earns respect.

It may seem like everything came easy to Bryant, but he spent countless hours behind the scenes working and practicing to be the best. Hard work may not always be seen, but it will earn the respect of others. That's important if you want to get ahead in life. As Bryant said, "I can't relate to lazy people."

3. Never give up.

You can't always win, but that doesn't mean you should just give up. Bryant once said, "The moment you give up is the moment you let someone else win." Never give up, because you never know what could happen.

4. Make the most of every situation.

As a young basketball player, it was challenging for Kobe to move to Italy. However, he found time to practice, got his grandfather to send him copies of games, and even got a job with the local basketball team, allowing him to grab some practice on the court. In short, he made the most of what he had.

5. Don't be afraid to fail.

Bryant once said, "If you're afraid to fail, then you're probably going to fail." Many people have found this to be true. Failing is a good way of learning and something you should never be afraid of.

STEPHEN CURRY
THE SPLASH BROTHER'S
REVOLUTIONARY IMPACT

Wardell Stephen Curry II was born on March 14, 1988, in Akron, Ohio. At the time, his father, Dell Curry, was a player for the NBA basketball team the Cleveland Cavaliers. When he retired in 2002, he was the all-time points leader for the Charlotte Hornets.

As a youngster, Curry and his brother Seth would often go to their father's basketball games. They would even shoot hoops with him during warmups. That may be why both brothers became NBA basketball players!

A brief move to Toronto near the end of his father's career saw young Stephen play for the Queensway Christian College boys basketball team. His efforts as a point guard helped the team complete the entire season undefeated! At the same time, he played for the Toronto 5-0. This team played against other teams across Ontario, and brought Curry into contact with Cory Joseph and Kelly Olynyk, both of whom were destined for the NBA. Curry helped Toronto 5-0 log a 33-4 season record and win a provincial championship.

Curry then headed back to Charlotte, as his dad had retired. He joined the Charlotte Christian School and led the school team to three conference titles. Thanks to Davidson College's aggressive pursuit of his talent, Curry then elected to attend their college and play for their team. He didn't disappoint! In his first season, he averaged 21.5 points per game and was the second-highest freshman scorer in the country. In his sophomore year, he was the main reason that the school made the NCAA tournament and they nearly won the tournament.

In 2009, Curry was the seventh overall pick in the NBA Draft and signed with the Golden State Warriors. The team already had Monta Ellis, a lean offensive point guard. Since both he and Curry were pretty thin, the coach decided they couldn't play together, so they had to share time on the court. But this didn't stop Curry from winning the Rookie of the Month award from the Western Conference in January, March, and April, and finishing runner-up position in the NBA Rookie of the Year award. He also set several records during his first year, including scoring 30+ points eight times in the season. This was the most 30-point games by any rookie that year, and the most since the great LeBron James logged 13. Curry even tied Michael Jordan for the second most 30-point/10-assist games as a rookie.

This was the start of an illustrious career with the Golden State Warriors, a team Curry has yet to leave. During his time, he has won four NBA championships, been the NBA finals MVP, won two NBA Most Valuable Player awards, and had 10 NBA All-Star appearances. He was crucial to the Warriors winning back-to-back NBA titles in 2017 and 2018, and the team also reached the NBA finals in 2019, where they lost to the Toronto Raptors.

Curry has put in a number of particularly noteworthy performances during his career, including his 54-point game against the New York Knicks on February 27, 2013. The game was held at Madison Square Garden, where Curry sank 11 three-pointers, setting a new franchise record and helping him to an impressive points total. The only players who have scored more than 54 points at Madison Square Gardens since 1968 are Kobe Bryant in 2009 and Michael Jordan in 1995!

On the last night of the regular 2012-2013 season, Curry sank a three-pointer with just seconds left in the second quarter. This basket gave him 270 three-pointers for the season, surpassing the previous record of 269 set by Allen in 2005-2006. That year, he was also the first player in NBA history to have at least 250 three-pointers and 500 assists in a single season!

If that wasn't enough, the following season (2014-2015), he ended the year with 286 three-pointers and helped the Warriors win 67 games and their first NBA title in 40 years! He also managed to score at least one three-pointer in 79 of his 80 games. In addition, he became the first player in NBA history to register multiple games with at least 50 points and 10 three-pointers. The next year, he took things to another level, becoming the first unanimous MVP winner in NBA history!

Curry has also been part of the American basketball squad. He first played for the US U-19 squad in the 2007 FIBA Under-19 World Championship. The team took silver, an indication of what was to come. In 2010, he joined the senior squad and played in the 2010 FIBA World Championship. The US had an undefeated run, winning the championship. He then helped the team repeat that feat in 2014 at the 2014 World Cup, and would have been part of the 2016 Olympic team, but had to withdraw due to injury.

Curry is considered one of the greatest players the NBA has ever seen, and the best shooter ever. People have said that he did for the three-pointer what Michael Jordan did for the slam dunk. He and his fellow "Splash Brother" Klay Thomson are also considered to be one of the best backcourt duos in NBA history, and have set a number of NBA records for three-pointers by a pair of teammates. That's quite a legacy for a player who has yet to hang up his boots!

FUN FACTS ABOUT STEPHEN CURRY

1. Since 2012, Curry has donated three insecticide-treated mosquito nets to the United Nations Foundations Nothing but Nets campaign to combat malaria every time he makes a three-pointer.
2. He's terrified of snakes.
3. Curry has nominated Denzel Washington to play him if there is ever a movie made about his life.
4. As a kid, he starred in a Burger King commercial.
5. Curry's sister, Sydel, played volleyball at Elon University.

QUICK TRIVIA TEST

1. What is Curry's full name?

Wardell Stephen Curry II.

2. What is Curry's younger brother's name, and what does he do?

Seth plays for the Charlotte Hornets.

3. Which year did Curry enter the NBA Draft?

2009.

4. How many NBA championships has he won?

Four.

5. When did the Warriors win back-to-back NBA championships with Curry?

2017 and 2018.

FIVE LIFE LESSONS

1. You can always do more!

Curry started setting new records practically from the start of his career. However, at no point has he said "that's enough." His passion for the game drives him forward, constantly improving himself and his game to do more.

2. Look after others.

Curry is actively involved with several charities, including the Nothing but Nets campaign. He believes in using his money and influence to help others. You may not have money or influence, but that doesn't stop you from looking after others.

3. If you want to succeed, work hard.

Curry once said, "Success is not an accident, success is a choice." This is something he lives by. Curry embraces the fact that success only happens when you work hard to be the best you can be, regardless of your level of talent.

4. Be confident.

Curry once said, "I have this irrational confidence in the shots I take." Of course, his skill backs up his confidence, but having that confidence allows him to take shots and get to the basket more often than not. We all need that same level of confidence in life.

5. Focus on those you care about.

Curry once said, "Honestly, I couldn't care less about other people's opinions of me." It's important not to spend time worrying about what others think. Instead, be true to your values and take care of those you care about. You simply can't please everyone, and you'll waste time and energy trying to please those you don't know.

ISIAH THOMAS
THE DETROIT PISTONS' FLOOR GENERAL

Isiah Lord Thomas III is often referred to by his nickname, Zeke. He was born April 30, 1961, in Chicago, Illinois, and grew up on the west side of the city, which had become a desirable destination for Black people migrating up from the South. The area was vibrant and thriving, although it suffered severe damage in the 1968 riots following the death of Martin Luther King.

Thomas's father had served in the US Armed Forces and was injured in the Battle of Saipan, but that didn't stop him from returning to trade school and eventually becoming the first Black supervisor at the International Harvester in Chicago. Unfortunately, he lost his job when the plant closed, and eventually left the family while Thomas was still a youngster.

Thomas started to play basketball at the age of three. He would practice his dribbling and shooting skills as part of the halftime entertainment at Catholic Youth Organization games. By the time he reached high school, he was an extremely talented player. Despite his high school being a 90-minute commute from home, he led the team to the state finals in his junior year.

There were several offers on the table when it came time for college, and Thomas and his mother chose the Indiana Hoosiers. She felt it would be good for him to get away from Chicago, and the coach, Bob Knight, was famous for his discipline, which she felt would be beneficial for Thomas.

As it turned out, she was right. Thomas had to quickly adjust because Knight made it clear from the start that no player, regardless of how good they were, was bigger than the team. Initial clashes got Thomas kicked out of practice, and Knight even threatened to put him on a plane home. This forced Thomas to buckle down and taught him valuable life lessons.

Fortunately, Thomas's skills and newfound temperament made him a favorite with Knight and the Indiana fans. In fact, Knight even adjusted his coaching style to make the most of Thomas's abilities! The two became friends as Thomas led the team to win two conference titles and the 1981 NCAA tournament.

In 1981, Thomas was the second overall pick in the NBA Draft. The Detroit Pistons offered him a four-year contract. This was the start of a 13-year playing career in which he stayed with the Pistons the entire time.

Thomas started his NBA career well, notably scoring 47 points on December 13, 1983, against the Denver Nuggets. He was also instrumental in the Piston's campaign against the New York Knicks in the 1984 NBA Playoffs. In a critical fifth game, he scored 16 points in just 94 seconds, forcing the game into overtime. Unfortunately, he ultimately fouled out and the Knicks won.

The Pistons reached the playoffs again in 1985, where they faced off against the Celtics. Unfortunately, the Celtics had Larry Bird, Kevin McHale, Robert Parish, and Dennis Johnson. Even with Thomas, the Pistons couldn't defeat them.

The Pistons faced the Celtics in the playoffs again in 1987, and lost again. To add insult to injury, the winning basket was a pass from Larry Bird to Dennis Johnson after Bird stole the ball from Thomas. But the following year, the Pistons got their revenge in the 1988 Eastern Conference Finals—the first finals for the

Pistons in 32 years. Interestingly, after losing, all of the Celtics players, with the exception of Kevin McHale, walked off the court without shaking hands.

The Pistons then faced the Lakers in the NBA title series. This was when Thomas and Magic Johnson memorably kissed each other on the cheek pre-game in a sign of their deep friendship. The series initially seemed to go in favor of the Pistons, and they had a 3-2 lead entering the sixth game. But late in the game, Thomas severely sprained his ankle. He hobbled through the rest of the game, but the Lakers ended up winning by one point. Thomas didn't recover fully for the seventh game, allowing the Lakers to take it 108-105.

Everything changed in the 1988-1989 season. Thomas and his teammates were nicknamed the Bad Boys, as they developed a brash and dominating style. It worked, and they swept through the playoffs, defeating the Celtics and then the Chicago Bulls. The Bulls had rising star Michael Jordan, who threatened to derail their campaign, but the Pistons utilized a specially devised strategy, nicknamed the Jordan Rules, to minimize his impact. They ultimately defeated the Bulls in six games, setting up a rematch with the Lakers in the NBA finals. This time, they won in four games, claiming the NBA championships.

Impressively, they repeated this success the following season, defeating the Knicks, Pacers, and Bulls in the playoffs and the Portland Trailblazers in the NBA championship series, where Thomas was voted the most valuable player.

This was Thomas's last great achievement, as the following season saw him and the team hit with a number of injuries. Injuries continued to plague Thomas over the next couple of years, and he eventually tore his Achilles tendon on April 19, 1994. A month later, he had no choice but to retire.

FUN FACTS ABOUT ISAIAH THOMAS

1. Thomas has the NBA record for most assists in a single NBA finals game—a staggering 25.
2. In 2003, he became the president of basketball operations for the New York Knicks.
3. He was named to the All-Star NBA team an impressive 12 times out of 13 seasons playing!
4. Thomas has won the NBA championship twice.
5. After retirement, he became a successful coach and sports analyst.

QUICK TRIVIA TEST

1. What did Thomas's college coach, Bob Knight, threaten to do?

Put him on a plane home.

2. What year did he enter the NBA Draft?

1981.

3. What year did the Pistons beat Celtics in the Eastern Conference finals?

1988.

4. What year did Thomas retire?

1994.

5. Why did he retire?

He failed to recover from a torn Achilles tendon.

FIVE LIFE LESSONS

1. Anything is possible.

Like many people of his era, Thomas didn't have the easiest start in life. His father left him, and his neighborhood was destroyed in the 1968 riots. But he didn't let this stop him from pursuing his dream and proving anything is possible.

2. Look for your opportunity.

There is little point in waiting and hoping you'll get a break. You need to look for any opportunity and make the most of it when you find it. As Thomas said, "Don't wait for opportunities to come to you. Seek them out."

3. Manners cost nothing.

The Celtics refusing to shake hands with the Pistons after losing to them in the NBA Final is an example of poor sportsmanship. Manners cost nothing, but the gesture is remembered long after. Remember that when dealing with people.

4. Friendship is more important than sport.

Magic Johnson and Thomas were friends, and they weren't afraid to show this friendship before they played against each other. It didn't stop them from being competitive, but it did show the importance of friendship.

5. You are more than one thing.

Thomas once said, "If all I'm remembered for is being a good basketball player, then I've done a bad job with the rest of my life." We are all the sum of everything we do, so we shouldn't be remembered or defined by one skill. Try hard at everything you do.

I have included these free downloadable gifts to help light up your inner inspiration & reach your potential.

While you are reading through the stories, lessons and trivia, we recommend that you make use of all the bonuses we've attached here!

All our bonuses have been made specifically to help young athletes feel fired up, get inspired from the best to ever do it, and most importantly fall more in love with this incredible game!

Here's a list of what you're getting:

1) 250 Fun Facts From The World Of Sports
2) Sports Practice and Game Calendar
3) 5 Fun Exercise Drills for Kids
4) The BEST Advice From The Greatest Athletes Of All Time
5) The Mental Mindset Guided Meditation & Affirmation Collection
6) The Most Famous Events In Sports History And What They Can Teach Us

Now, it's over to you to scan the QR code, follow the instructions & get started!

JOHN STOCKTON
THE ASSIST MAESTRO

John Houston Stockton was born on March 26, 1962, in Spokane, Washington. His childhood was relatively unremarkable, in that it was pretty normal and even ideal. Stockton had two devoted parents (Clementine and Jack) and plenty of friends, and attended St. Aloysius grade school. He then moved to Gonzaga Prep High School, where he graduated in 1980. Naturally, his skills as a basketball player were already established by then. In fact, while at high school, he broke the record for most points scored in a basketball season.

His skill on the court led to offers from several universities. Ultimately, Stockton decided to stay in Spokane and attended Gonzaga University. He played for the university team (known as the Bulldogs), becoming the third generation in his family to attend the university. In fact, his grandfather had been a well-known player at the university in the 1920s.

Stockton's skills helped the Bulldogs thrive. During his senior year in 1984, he averaged 20.9 points per game, with 57% of his shots coming from the field. The team achieved a 17-11 record, which was the best they had done in 17 years! This earned Stockton the WCAC Player of the Year.

When Bob Knight invited him to try out for the 1984 US Olympic team, Stockton was one of just 74 players invited. He made the final 20, but was released in May.

Also in 1984, Stockton entered the NBA Draft, where he was selected by the Utah Jazz in the first round. Despite nearly making the Olympic team, he was a relative unknown and his arrival was a shock to the Jazz fans. They soon warmed to him, however, especially when Stockton scored 19 points in 19 minutes against the Denver Nuggets. The Jazz ended up losing the game, but it showed what Stockton could do, and he quickly became the team's starting point guard.

Despite having a good season and being 10th in the MVP voting, Stockton was only named to the All-NBA Second Team and wasn't selected to play in the 1988 NBA All-Star Game. This oversight was corrected the following season, when he made the All-Star Team and had more assists than anyone else in the NBA.

His form continued, and on January 15, 1991, he scored 20 points in one game (a career-high), alongside a record-breaking 28 assists. Stockton then helped Jazz reach the Western Conference Finals in 1992. This was a real accomplishment, since it was the first time the team had made it this far. Unfortunately, they were ultimately defeated by the Portland Trail Blazers.

During the 1994-1995 season, Stockton achieved a number of major milestones. At the beginning of February 1995, he slipped past Magic Johnson to take the NBA record for number of assists. To cement this, he added 16 more assists in the Jazz's defeat of the visiting Denver Nuggets, taking his career assist total to 9,937. Before the end of the month, Stockton had helped in the defeat of the Celtics, adding another 15 assists to his total and taking him past 10,000. He was the first player in NBA history to achieve this. That same year, he passed the 2,000 mark for steals, becoming the second player in the history of the NBA to do so.

The Jazz continued to perform well, and reached the Western Conference Finals again in the 1996-97 season. This was another chance for Stockton to shine. In the sixth game of the conference finals, he scored 25 points, with a buzzer-beater three-point shot over the head of Charles Barkley giving the Jazz a win and propelled the team to the finals. That basket subsequently became known as "The Shot." Unfortunately, Michael Jordan and the Chicago Bulls were too much for the Jazz in the Finals.

Amazingly, both teams repeated their dominance the next year and met again in the 1997-98 Finals. Again, the Bulls won, but only just.

On May 2, 2003, Stockton announced he would be retiring. He ended his 19-season career with the Jazz at the peak of his powers, and was content with his performance. He simply felt it was time to see more of his family. The Jazz retired his number 12 jersey, and there is now a statue of him in front of the Delta Centre, along with one of Karl Malone.

After retiring, Stockton moved back to Spokane and started coaching youth teams. In 2003, he was an assistant on eight different teams! The Jazz also personally invited him to train Deron Williams and Trey Burke.

Later in his career, Stockton released an autobiography and became an assistant coach for Montana State University's women's basketball program, maintaining his influence in the game that he loved.

FUN FACTS ABOUT JOHN STOCKTON

1. Stockton is regarded as one of the greatest point guards in NBA history.
2. He played 1,504 out of a possible 1,526 games in his career, showcasing how resilient he was.
3. His final tally of career assists was 15,806. That's an NBA record that is unlikely to be broken.
4. His teamwork with Karl Malone created one of the most lethal combinations in NBA history.
5. Stockton was inducted into the Naismith Memorial Basketball Hall of Fame in 2009.

QUICK TRIVIA TEST

1. What is Stockton's full name?

John Houston Stockton.

2. What year did he enter the NBA Draft?

1984.

3. Which year did he set the NBA record for assists?

1995.

4. What else did he achieve that same year?

Became the second player in the history of the NBA to get over 2,000 steals.

5. What number jersey did he wear with the Jazz?

12.

FIVE LIFE LESSONS

1. Never quit!

Stockton once said, "The only place success comes before work is in the dictionary." You can't be successful unless you're prepared to put in the work. He certainly was.

2. Be consistent.

It can sometimes be hard to find what you're really good at. However, if you aim to be consistent in everything you do, it can lead to great things. Stockton illustrated this perfectly. While he was more than capable of scoring baskets, his true talent was in consistently providing the assist. He established a reputation for it, and set an NBA record that may never be beaten!

3. Lead by example.

Stockton once said, "Leadership is not about being in charge." It's about setting an example and knowing that others will follow. Stockton was very good at doing this, but it is something we all can do.

4. You can't always win.

No one wins every time—and that's okay. You need to learn to deal with failure and use it to help you improve. As Stockton said, "Success is not final, failure is not fatal. It is the courage to continue that counts."

5. Work on your attitude.

Stockton once said, "Excellence is not a skill. It is an attitude." In other words, you don't need great talent to excel, but you do need to adopt the mindset of excellence in everything you do. The rest will take care of itself.

ALLEN IVERSON
THE ANSWER'S UNDENIABLE IMPACT

Allen Ezail Iverson was born on June 7, 1975, in Hampton, Virginia. He was raised by his mother. Even though his father wasn't present, Iverson still had male influences in his life. Michael Freeman was his main father figure until he was arrested in front of 13-year-old Iverson for dealing drugs. This caused Iverson to act up at school, take unauthorized absences, and ultimately fail the eighth grade. Before all of this happened, he had been known for looking out for younger kids.

Iverson eventually made it through eighth grade and enrolled at Bethel High School. He was accepted onto the football team, where he played quarterback, running back, kick returner, and defensive back. Because he was naturally athletic, he also signed up as a point guard for the school basketball team. Impressively, he led the football team and basketball team to victory in the Virginia State Championships. This earned him the Associated Press High School Player of the Year award.

Despite appearances, Iverson still didn't have his life together. A shouting match between his friend group and another group of young people in the local bowling alley led to a fight, where Iverson was alleged to have struck a woman in the head with a chair. Iverson and three of his friends were arrested, and he spent four months in a local correctional facility. Interestingly, a videotape later surfaced, showing him leaving as the fighting began, but the conviction wasn't overturned until 1995.

Iverson states that his jail experience helped him learn to be strong. He refused to show any weakness, or to be exploited. Of course, the experience threatened to derail his promising sports career, as he had to finish high school at Richard Milburn High School. Fortunately, his display of skill at Bethel had convinced Georgetown University's coach to meet him and offer him a scholarship.

Iverson was finally on the right path, and in his first year of college he won the Rookie of the Year award. He averaged 20.4 points per game and took the team to the Sweet 16 round of the NCAA tournament. The following year, he led the team to the Big East championship and the elite eight round of the NCAA tournament. He then declared for the NBA Draft early in 1996.

Despite a rocky road to success, Iverson was selected first overall in the 1996 NBA Draft by the Philadelphia 76ers. At just 6 feet tall, he was the shortest ever first-round pick. The Philadelphia 76ers weren't doing well—the previous season they'd had an 18-64 record. But Iverson was instrumental in turning this around. In his debut game, he scored 30 points, matching Willie Anderson for the third-highest scoring output by a rookie. A month later, he topped that performance with 35 points. But it was a game against the Chicago Bulls that really fired him up. Iverson managed to execute a perfect crossover in front of Michael Jordan, wrong-footing him and helping Iverson score a record-breaking minimum of 40 points in five consecutive games. He was named the Rookie of the Year, and the Sixers improved to a 22-60.

The following season, the team got a new coach and some additional talent, and managed a 31-51 record. This is when

Iverson and his fellow guard Larry Hughes earned the nickname "The Flight Brothers," as they consistently played above the rim.

The 1998-99 season saw Iverson log a 26.8-point average per game, better than anyone else in the league. The Sixers finally won more than they lost, finishing the lockout season with a 28-22 record. This was also the first time Iverson was named to the All-NBA First Team.

While his crossover against Michael Jordan was memorable, it wasn't the only impressive move he made while helping the Sixers improve their record. Iverson's skills also gave him nearly 2,000 steals, over 5,600 assists, and an impressive 24,000 points over 14 years on the court. He started 901 out of a possible 914 games and featured on the All-Star Team 11 times.

One example of his most impressive plays came against the Wizards in November 2004. There were just 3.3 seconds left on the clock, and the teams were tied, 114 points each. It was time for Iverson to do what he did best. He stole the ball on an inbound pass and steamed up the right side of the court to lay the ball straight into the net. With just two-tenths of a second left, the Wizards had no time to respond—the win went to the Sixers.

Iverson ended his legendary career with 11 All-Star performances, seven All-NBA awards, four scoring titles, and five seasons with a 30+ point average. The only thing he never accomplished was winning a championship. Because he helped turn things around for the Sixers, he became known as "The Answer"—the answer to all of their problems!

FUN FACTS ABOUT ALLEN IVERSON

1. Iverson almost played football for Notre Dame instead of basketball.
2. He once unintentionally pranked his coach Larry Hughes.
3. He's an avid cartoonist!
4. Iverson completed 40 dunks in his NBA career, despite being only 6 feet tall.
5. Hoop Magazine once airbrushed his tattoos off.

QUICK TRIVIA TEST

1. What is Iverson's full name?

Allen Ezail Iverson.

2. What year did he enter the NBA Draft?

1996.

3. How many steals did he get in his career?

Over 2,000.

4. How many seasons did he play in the NBA?

14.

5. Why did Iverson go to jail?

For allegedly hitting someone with a chair.

FIVE LIFE LESSONS

1. Never quit!

Many players can attest to the power of not quitting. However, it's particularly relevant for Iverson. His career was nearly derailed by a false allegation that saw him serve four months in jail. Fortunately for the sport and the Sixers, he didn't quit.

2. Be true to yourself.

Iverson was well known for his cornrows and his alternative dress style (which later became popular in the league). He also famously got upset when Hoop Magazine airbrushed his tattoos off. As he said, "Hey, I am who I am." This is good advice—you should be who you are.

3. No matter how good you are, you still need to practice.

Iverson once said, "When you are not practicing, someone else is getting better." If you want to be the best, you have to keep practicing.

4. You can't always win.

Iverson once said, "I failed, got back up. I failed, got back up." The truth is, you can't always win, and you will definitely fail sometimes. What matters is what you do afterward. Get back up, learn from the failure, and try again.

5. Do it your own way.

Iverson was unique. He played the game his way, and was successful because he did so. That's a good attitude to have. As he once said, "I don't want to be another Jordan, Magic, or Isaiah. When my career is over, I want to be able to look in the mirror and say 'I did it my way.'"

DWYANE WADE
THE FLASH'S IMPACT

Dwayne Tyrone Wade Jr was born on January 17, 1982, in Chicago, Illinois. He was the second of two children, although he also had two step-siblings from his mother's past relationship. Dwayne's real father left his mother when he was just four months old.

Unfortunately, his mother struggled with drug addiction and often committed crimes to feed her habit. When Wade was eight, his older sister tricked him, making him think they were going to the movies. Instead, they went to live with his father and stepmother. For a while, Wade would visit his mother, but then his father moved them all to Robbins, Illinois, and Wade didn't see his mother again for two years.

Wade was faced with two options: sports or a life of drugs and gangs. He threw himself into sports—specifically basketball and football. He credits his sister for pointing him in the right direction—that and his idolization of Michael Jordan.

When he enrolled at Harold L. Richards High School, he joined the basketball and football teams. He was immediately seen as a great wide receiver and a useful backup quarterback, but he didn't have as much luck in basketball, due to his height. However, by his sophomore year, he had grown four inches. He became the team leader and scored an average of 20.7 points per game. The following year, he did even better, setting school records for points and steals and leading the team to a 24-5 record and an appearance at the Class AA Eisenhower Sectionals. His ACT scores were low, however, so only Marquette, Illinois State, and DePaul recruited him to play college basketball.

Wade chose to go to Marquette, but was unable to play during his freshman year because his academic record wasn't good enough. (NCAA Proposition 48 sets academic standards for participation in division sports.) With the help of a tutor, he dedicated the year to improving his academics, ensuring him a place on the basketball squad for his sophomore year.

That year, he was eager to make up for lost time and led the Marquette Golden Eagles to a 26-7 record, their best since the 1993-1994 season. He averaged 17.8 points per game and led Conference USA in steals and field goals. In his junior year at Marquette, he led the team to a 27-6 record and scored an impressive average of 21.5 points per game. He was instrumental in taking the team to the Final Four of the national championship, the first time they had gotten that far since 1977. The team also won the Conference USA title. Wade's performance was so good that he earned an NBA Draft projection and decided to skip his final year to enter the 2003 NBA Draft.

Wade was selected fifth in the draft by the Miami Heat, making him the highest-ranked Marquette first-round pick ever. It was immediately obvious that he was a good investment. He quickly averaged 16.2 points per game, with a 46.5% shooting average. While the Heat started the season slowly, by the end, they had achieved a respectable 42-40 record and qualified for the playoffs. Thanks in part to his consistent performance, as well as his impressive postseason stats, Wade received a unanimous selection to the 2004 NBA All-Rookie team and placed third in the Rookie of the Year award. He also led his team in assists and points in the postseason, making him only the fourth rookie to ever do so!

A few changes to the team led to a fantastic season for Wade in 2004-05. The team improved to 59-23 for the season and hit the playoffs with style, sweeping the New Jersey Nets, then dispatching the Washington Wizards to meet the Detroit Pistons in the Finals. They lost the series 3-4, but it could have been very different if Wade hadn't strained a rib muscle, which stopped him from playing the sixth game and only allowed for limited play in the seventh.

The team made up for it in the 2006 playoffs, although Wade once again encountered a series of injuries. Fortunately, he was able to play through them and helped the team beat the Chicago Bulls and the Detroit Pistons, setting up a Finals clash with the Dallas Mavericks. Wade's impressive points totals in games 3, 4, and 5 (42, 36, and 43, respectively) took the Heat from a 0-2 deficit to winning the series 4-2. Wade won the Finals MVP trophy and his team took the championship.

Wade continued to play well, and stayed with the Miami Heat until 2016—a total of 13 seasons. In 2016, he spent a season with the Chicago Bulls before moving to the Cleveland Cavaliers for a year. He then spent his last season back with the Miami Heat. It was fitting that his return to the Heat coincided with him reaching a total of 20,000 points and 5,000 assists.

Although he retired at the end of the season, he went out on a high, passing Larry Bird to become 10th on the NBA career postseason scoring list and leading the Heat in breaking the Philadelphia 76er's 17-game winning streak.

FUN FACTS ABOUT DWAYNE WADE

1. Wade was given the nickname "The Flash" by his teammate Shaquille O'Neal to highlight the fact that he liked to make flashy moves. The nickname stuck!
2. He chose his jersey number 3 in honor of the Holy Trinity.
3. Throughout his career, he donated 10% of his salary to charity.
4. He was selected for the NBA All-Star Team 13 times out of 16 playing seasons.
5. Wade has his own line of sneakers in conjunction with the Li-Ning brand.

QUICK TRIVIA TEST

1. What's Wade's full name?

Dwayne Tyrone Wade Jr.

2. When was Wade born?

January 17, 1982.

3. Who did Wade idolize growing up?

Michael Jordan.

4. Why did he not play basketball during his freshman year of college?

His academic scores were too low.

5. Which year did he enter the NBA Draft?

2003.

FIVE LIFE LESSONS

1. There is always a way forward.

When things look bleak and there seems to be no way to move toward your goal, remember that Wade faced his own set of challenges at college. Unable to play due to a poor academic record, he knuckled down and improved his grades, allowing him to play on the team and excel at what he does best.

2. It's okay to be a showman.

People often frown at those who are a little too flashy, perhaps even calling them show-offs. However, if you have the talent and have worked hard to build your skills, there's no harm in adding a little panache to your activities. It can help you gain recognition, and is how Wade earned his nickname.

3. Set your own goals.

Wade once said, "Success means being satisfied with what you do every day. It's being proud of the better person you are becoming." The only person you have to make proud of is yourself. Set your own goals, work toward them, and be proud when you achieve them.

4. Don't be afraid to speak up.

Wade once said, "The biggest thing is to let your voice be heard, let your story be heard." That's good advice, and something he lives by today. Your opinion matters, so speak up and let others hear what you have to say.

5. Success comes when you least expect it.

Wade was nearing retirement after a rocky last couple of years. He returned to the Heat for one more season and reached several milestones, including his overall point score and assists. You never know when success will happen, so do your best and live in the moment.

CLYDE DREXLER
GLIDE'S FLIGHT TO SUCCESS

Clyde Austin Drexler was born on June 22, 1962, in New Orleans, Louisiana, but he grew up in South Park, Houston, Texas, and attended Ross Sterling High School. While he was naturally athletic, his path to the NBA wasn't as smooth as many of the greats. Drexler tried out for the varsity basketball team when he was a sophomore, but wasn't deemed to be good enough for the team. He finally made the team his senior year, and played center. Being 6 feet 6 inches helped! However, the real reason he made the team was because he practiced. His skills had improved, and his performance against Sharpstown High School in the 1979 Christmas tournament got him noticed. In that one game, he logged 34 points and 27 rebounds, which was enough to get college coaches looking at him.

Drexler received offers from New Mexico State University, Texas Tech University, and the University of Houston. The Houston offer was a direct result of his friend, Michael Young, telling the school that Drexler was the best player he had ever played against. Drexler eventually chose Houston because he could stay at home and be with his friend, Young (whom the school also recruited).

Because Drexler was still relatively unknown, the decision by Houston coach Guy Lewis to let him play was met with hate mail from Houston supporters and alumni. They had already decided Drexler wasn't good enough. How wrong they were!

Drexler, his friend Young, Larry Micheaux, and Hakeem Olajuwon collectively became known as the "Phi Slama Jama," thanks to their acrobatic, frequently above-the-rim style of play. This was also why Drexler became known as Clyde the Glide.

In 1982, Houston made it to the Final Four, where they lost to the eventual champions. The following season, they returned as the favorites and narrowly missed out on taking the championship. During this tournament Sports Illustrated writer Curry Kirkpatrick called Drexler's double-pump slam "your basic play of the century."

Drexler declared himself ready for the NBA Draft, leaving Houston as the Southwestern Conference Player of the Year. To this day, his 268 steals for Houston have not been beaten. He's also the only player in the history of the school to gain over 1,000 career points, 900 rebounds, and 300 assists.

Drexler was selected by the Portland Trail Blazers in the 1983 NBA Draft, where he was the 14th overall pick. This was the start of a 12-year relationship with the team, one that would carry him to the heights of NBA stardom.

In 1990, Drexler led the Trail Blazers to the Conference Finals. Although he was only the top scorer in two games, he was instrumental in the team making it to the championships for the first time since 1977. Unfortunately, while Drexler scored two impressive free throws with 2.1 seconds left to beat the Detroit Pistons, that was the only game of the final series they won.

Drexler had to wait until 1995 to get his NBA championship. This was after he transferred to the Houston Rockets, because Portland was no longer a serious contender. Drexler and his teammate Olajuwon propelled the Rockets through the playoffs and into the finals, where they mopped the floor with the Orlando

Magic. It was the third time Drexler played in the NBA finals, and this time he averaged 21.5 points per game.

Drexler was nominated to the NBA All-Star team 10 times in his career. In 1992, he also made the All-NBA First Team. During his career, he earned 22,195 points, with a points-per-game average of 20.4. He also had 6,677 rebounds and 6,125 assists.

After retiring in 1998, he became head coach for the men's basketball team at the University of Houston, where he spent years giving back to the sport.

FUN FACTS ABOUT CLYDE DREXLER

1. In high school, Drexler was classmates with tennis star Zina Garrison.
2. Drexler entered the Texas Sports Hall of Fame in 1998 and the Houston Sports Hall of Fame in 2022.
3. In 2007, he was a contestant on Dancing with the Stars. Unfortunately, he was eliminated in the fourth week of the competition.
4. When he left the Trail Blazers, he had the all-time scoring record of 18,040 points, which wasn't broken until 2022.
5. He has four children: Erica, Austin, Elise, and Adam

QUICK TRIVIA TEST

1. What is Drexler's full name?

Clyde Austin Drexler.

2. What was the tournament that got Drexler noticed by colleges?

The 1979 Christmas Tournament, specifically the match against the Sharpstown High School.

3. Which year did he enter the NBA Draft?

1983.

4. What year did he finally become an NBA champion?

1995.

5. What was his nickname?

Clyde the Glide.

FIVE LIFE LESSONS

1. Never stop practicing.

If you're good at something, you may feel like you don't need to practice. Likewise, if you've reached the pinnacle of your career, you may feel practice is no longer necessary. Drexler learned as a youngster that you can't stop practicing. It's the reason he made the team his senior year, and the reason he consistently improved throughout his career.

2. Ignore the haters.

Taylor Swift famously said, "Haters are going to hate." This is true in all walks of life—and in most cases, haters don't even need a genuine reason to hate. The best thing you can do is ignore them and focus on your goals. That's what Drexler did when he started with Houston.

3. Work hard to win at anything.

Drexler once said, "Hard work beats talent when talent doesn't work hard." The truth is, no matter how great your talent is, you can't turn it into a winning force without working at it. That's the only way to learn and improve, making your talent a usable skill and building a pathway to success

4. Patience is a virtue.

Drexler had to wait over a decade to finally win an NBA championship. He even had to switch teams to make it happen. His patience, hard work, and dedication were eventually rewarded when he won the championship in 1995.

5. Remember that you're a role model.

You may not realize it, but there will be times when others will look up to you and emulate you. Drexler put it well when he said, "I don't care what anybody says: A pro athlete is going to be a role model. I tried to use that as a positive influence, to let kids know we are regular people." It doesn't matter what field you do well in, success will make you a role model. Try to keep that in mind.

CHRIS PAUL
THE POINT GOD'S LEADERSHIP

Chris Emanuel Paul was born on May 6, 1985, in Winston-Salem, North Carolina. His older brother was named Charles Paul, and his father was also named Charles Paul. This led to him being given the nickname CP3, since all three men in his family had the same initials. His father was known as CP1 and his brother was CP2.

As a youngster growing up in Lewisville, he spent a lot of time playing basketball and football with his brother and dad. His father had been an athlete and was keen to integrate fitness and athleticism into his son's routines. This led to him coaching both the Paul brothers in a variety of youth leagues. The boys also worked in their grandfather's service station during the summers. Paul often refers to his grandfather as his "best friend," and says many of the life lessons he learned came from him.

Paul went to West Forsyth High School, where he played on the junior varsity team during his freshman and sophomore years. During his junior year, he averaged 25 points per game and was key to the team reaching the semifinals. In his senior year, he played for the senior team and drew a lot of attention when he scored 61 points in a single game. Paul dedicated the game to his grandfather, who had been murdered earlier in the year— scoring one point for each year his grandfather was alive. That season, he averaged 30.8 points per game.

He had several college offers, but ultimately chose Wake Forest University. As a freshman, he averaged 14.8 points per game and set school freshman records for three-point percentage, free throws, free throw percentage, assists, and steals! Thanks to his efforts, the team made the Sweet Sixteen of the NCAA tournament, and he was named ACC Rookie of the Year. The following year, he led the team to the second round of the NCAA tournament and a surprise defeat to West Virginia.

In 2005, he made himself available for the NBA draft and announced his intent to go professional. The New Orleans Hornets took Paul as the fourth overall pick in the draft. However, that year the majority of the team's games were played in Oklahoma City, because of the damage caused by Hurricane Katrina. Paul led the rookies in his first season, and became the second rookie in NBA history to lead the league in total steals. His points-per-game average of 16.1 helped him secure the NBA Rookie of the Year award.

Paul was instrumental in the Hornet's success over the following two years. By 2007, they were near the top of the Western Conference standings and finished the season with 56 wins, which was a new franchise record.

The following year illustrated why basketball is a team sport. Paul improved his average to a healthy 22.8 per game, but the team struggled and didn't produce as good a record as the season before. They were eliminated in the first round of the NBA playoffs.

The 2009-2010 season was challenging for Paul. A slow start led to his coach, Bryon Scott, being replaced. Paul didn't approve of this, and even commented that the team management should have consulted him first. That same season, in early February 2010, Paul tore cartilage in his left knee, which put him out of action for a month. He missed the All-Star Game and his average dropped to 18.7 per game. The Hornets struggled as a result of Paul missing a large chunk of the season.

The following season, Paul collided with a Cavaliers player in a game. This resulted in him being carried off the court on a stretcher. He suffered a concussion, which knocked him out for two games. However, he played the rest of the season and helped carry the Hornets to the playoffs. Despite exceptional play, the team was eliminated and Paul started to look elsewhere.

Paul never managed to secure an NBA championship, but he played for a number of teams and set a bunch of records, demonstrating that he deserved to win, over and over again. For the 2019-2020 season, he returned to Oklahoma City. This was the first time he found himself on a young team without any hope of a championship. Despite this, he took on a role as a veteran leader and helped the young team reach the fifth seed in the Western Conference. This meant Oklahoma had to play Paul's previous team, the Rockets, in the first round of the playoffs. Due to his performance, the series went to seven games, with Oklahoma just barely losing. Sports Illustrated stated that Paul had reestablished himself as one of the best point guards in the NBA, and his time at Oklahoma was a success.

Paul also played for the national team. His first appearance was in the 2006 FIBA World Championship, where his 44 assists (the highest in the tournament) helped the USA win bronze. He also played for the US in the 2008 Olympics, where they won every game to earn gold. They then repeated this feat in the 2012 Olympics, with Paul as the starting point guard.

Today, Paul plays for the Golden State Warriors. He is still at the top of his game, and has earned the nickname "The Point God" to go along with his original nickname, CP3.

FUN FACTS ABOUT CHRIS PAUL

1. He was president of the National Basketball Players Association from 2013 to 2021.
2. Paul is passionate about bowling. He is an expert bowler and owns a franchise in the Professional Bowler Association.
3. He started the CP3 Foundation to help those who suffered in Hurricane Katrina.
4. Paul was named to the NBA All-Star team 10 times.
5. He regularly appears in State Farm commercials as Cliff Paul and Cliff Paul's twin brother.

QUICK TRIVIA TEST

1. What is Paul's full name?

Chris Emanuel Paul.

2. Where was he born?

Winston-Salem, North Carolina.

3. What year did he enter the NBA?

2005.

4. What Injury did he suffer after playing the Cavaliers?

Concussion.

5. What foundation did he start?

CP3 Foundation, to help people affected by Hurricane Katrina.

FIVE LIFE LESSONS

1. Remember that you're part of a team.

When you have an enormous amount of talent, it can be difficult to remember the team that helped you get where you are. But in basketball, if you forget the team, your performance will suffer. That's what happened to Paul in his second season with the Hornets. In short, if you want to do well, play as part of the team.

2. Never give up.

Paul has suffered a variety of injuries in his career, many at inopportune times, potentially destroying his hopes of winning a championship. However, he never gave up and always returned to peak physical form. That's something everyone should strive to do in life.

3. Size doesn't matter.

Most basketball players are tall, and this is often a prerequisite for making a team. At 6 feet, Paul is considered small in the NBA. He doesn't let this affect him, though. He embraces it and uses it to his advantage. As he once said, "I'm a little brother. I've always been small. People have said I have a Napoleon complex. But I've always had to fight for everything that I have."

4. You can't always win.

Paul once said, "Every now and then, you're going to get beaten, but we work hard." Losing is part of playing the game. As long as you've worked hard and done your best, then there is no shame in losing. Learn a lesson and try again.

5. Be true to yourself.

Paul is known as a leader and a very vocal person, perhaps on account of his small stature. However, you don't have to copy his style to be a leader. Stay true to yourself and lead in your own way. As he says, "You don't always have to be a leader and be as vocal as I am. I'm sure some people would love it if I didn't talk as much as I did."

STEVE NASH
THE MAESTRO OF
BASKETBALL ARTISTRY

Stephen John Nash was born on February 7, 1974, in Johannesburg, South Africa. His mother was Welsh and his father was English. When he was just 18 months old, his family moved to Regina, Saskatchewan, Canada. Shortly after that, they moved again, this time to Victoria, British Columbia.

Before settling in Canada, Nash's father was a professional soccer player. This encouraged Nash and his younger brother to play soccer and Canada's favorite sport, ice hockey. His neighbors were future NHL stars Russ and Geoff Courtnall.

Nash didn't start playing basketball until he was 12 years old, and his competitive career only began when he enrolled at St. Michaels University school. It was a private school his parents put him in because his grades were dropping at Mount Douglas Secondary. He joined the basketball team at St. Michaels, in addition to playing soccer and rugby. In his senior season, he averaged 21.3 points per game and led the team to win the British Columbia AAA Provincial Championship. He was named Player of the Year.

Despite efforts by his high school coach, including sending 30 highlight reels to American universities, only Santa Clara coach Dick Davey came for a look at Nash. He was instantly sold on the young player, and nervous that someone else would see Nash's raw talent. Fortunately, no one else did, and Nash accepted a scholarship from Santa Clara.

In his first year, Nash led his new team to the NCAA finals and won. This was particularly impressive since they beat the number two seeded team in the finals. Meanwhile, the Santa Clara Broncos hadn't even been in the NCAA tournament for five years! To add icing to the cake, Nash scored six straight free throws in the last 30 seconds of the game.

The following season wasn't as successful. But then, in 1994-95, the Broncos topped the WCC, nearly won the NCAA tournament, and Nash was named Conference Player of the Year. Nash subsequently contemplated entering the NBA Draft in 1995. However, as he didn't feel he would be a first-round pick, so he decided against it. Instead, he spent the summer honing his skills playing with the Canadian national team.

The next year, he once again helped Santa Clara take the WCC title. When he was named Conference Player of the Year for the second consecutive season, the national media and scouts started to pay attention. By the time he had finished at Santa Clara, he was the school's all-time leader in assists (with 510), free throw percentage (0.862), and attempted three-pointers (263 for 656).

The following year, he entered the draft and was picked 15th overall by the Phoenix Suns. The Suns fans were not impressed, as they hadn't heard of him—and their attitude toward him didn't change quickly. Nash only played 10.5 minutes per game in his first season, since he was in a supporting role to established point guards Kevin Johnson, Sam Cassell, and Jason Kidd. In his second season, he fared slightly better, and even managed 13th in the league for his three-point field goal percentage.

After just two seasons, the Suns coach, Donnie Nelson, left to become assistant general manager of the Dallas Mavericks. He convinced the Mavericks to buy the underused Nash. It immediately became obvious that Nash was a formidable point guard, and with the Mavericks, he was allowed to start in all 40 games of the shortened lockout season. That first year with the team, he averaged 7.9 points and the Mavericks failed to make the playoffs. However, new ownership, additional talent, and a better atmosphere saw Nash and the team begin to thrive in the 1999-2000 season.

The following year, it all started to come together. The Mavericks made the Western Conference playoffs for the first time in over a decade. They lost in the semifinals, but it was the start of an impressive run for Nash and the team. In the 2001-2002 season, Nash averaged 17.9 points per game and 7.7 average assists. He earned his first NBA All-Star Game spot and was seen as part of the Mavericks "Big Three." The following season he again averaged around 17.7 points and 7.3 assists per game as the team made it all the way to the Western Conference finals.

Interestingly, Nash returned to the Suns in 2004 and spent eight years with them. When he arrived, they had just finished the season with 29 wins and 53 losses. Little was expected from the team the next year, but the new coach favored up-tempo games and needed athletic players. Nash excelled and helped the team earn a points-per-game average of 110.4, higher than it had been in a decade. They also finished the season with 62 wins and 20 losses. Nash also managed to win the 2004-05 NBA MVP Award and took the team all the way to the Western Conference finals for the first time since 1993.

Nash retired in 2015, after suffering a variety of issues over a number of years. In an effort to give something back to basketball, he signed with the Golden State Warriors as a part-time consultant. With his help, the Warriors had a record-breaking 73 wins to 9 losses and made the 2016 NBA finals, although they ultimately lost. They made up for it the following year when they beat the defending champions in the finals. This gave Nash his first NBA championship—although not as a player!

FUN FACTS ABOUT STEVE NASH

1. Nash is a British citizen and a Canadian citizen.
2. When he was eight years old, he told his mother he would play in the NBA.
3. Santa Clara retired his number 11 jersey in 2006. This was the first jersey the college ever retired.
4. He was inducted into the Basketball Hall of Fame in September 2018.
5. Nash won his first NBA championship as a consultant.

QUICK TRIVIA TEST

1. What's Nash's full name?

Stephen John Nash.

2. When was he born?

February 7, 1974.

3. Which year did he enter the NBA Draft?

1996.

4. What year did he get his first NBA championship win?

2017.

5. When did he earn his first NBA All-Star Team spot?

2002.

FIVE LIFE LESSONS

1. Believe in yourself.

Nash believed he was a great basketball player and deserved his spot in the NBA. Even when he had a slow start to his NBA career, he kept going until he had proven himself. You should do the same. Believe in yourself and great things will happen.

2. Think about others.

It may not have always been visible, but Nash constantly thought about others. This was showcased by his interactions with Dave Lewis. An initial interview by Lewis left Nash knowing more about Lewis than Lewis did about Nash! That knowledge meant that Nash always recognized and found time for Lewis, which meant a lot to him. Don't underestimate how you can positively affect others.

3. Lead by example.

Nash is often said to be the pioneer of the current team-based playing style, as opposed to the one-on-one style of the past. It wasn't a conscious decision by Nash to change the game—he simply played the game his way and led by example. This is often more effective than dictating what others do.

4. Play to your strengths.

In sports, life, and business, you will have strengths and weaknesses. Nash's great strength wasn't his accuracy at shooting, although he was quite good. Instead, it was his ability to get the best out of his teammates. You should recognize your own strengths and use them to help yourself and others.

5. Accept and use criticism.

People will criticize you, and you can either accept it and learn from it, or allow it to rile you up. The first choice is the best one. As Nash once said, "You should always want your coach to be critical. It gives you an opportunity to learn and to overcome adversity."

JASON KIDD
THE FLOOR GENERAL'S
BRILLIANCE

Jason Frederick Kidd was born on March 23, 1973, and would go on to become one of the greatest point guards of all time. He was born in San Francisco to an African-American father and an Irish-American mother. As a youngster, he spent a lot of time at the East Oakland Youth Development Center honing his skills on the court. Much of the time, he played against Gary Payton, who is now in the Basketball Hall of Fame.

Kidd attended St. Joesph Notre Dame High School in Alameda, where his talent was instantly spotted by Coach Frank LaPorte, who helped him become the best player possible. During his time at the school, he led the team to back-to-back victories in the state championship. His points-per-game average in his senior season was 25, and he also averaged 10 assists, seven rebounds, and seven steals per game. Unsurprisingly, he won the first of many trophies that year—the Naismith Award for the nation's top high school player.

A host of universities offered Kidd scholarships, but he shocked everyone by choosing the University of California, Berkeley. It was nearby, but its basketball team was stuck in a rut. The team had just had a 10-18 losing season, and hadn't won a conference title since 1960!

Kidd quickly set about turning this around. He averaged 13 points per and 3.8 steals per game in his first season. A total of 110 steals in the season gave him the NCAA record for most steals as a freshman, and he helped the Golden Bears reach the NCAA Sweet 16, where they lost to Kansas.

Kidd continued to lift the Golden Bears as a sophomore, again taking them to the NCAA tournament, although this time they were knocked out in the first round. He then opted to enter the NBA draft in 1994.

Kidd was the second overall pick in the 1994 draft and made an instant impact with his new team, the Dallas Mavericks. In his first season, he averaged 11.7 points per game and led the NBA in triple doubles. He was named the 1995 Rookie of the Year, an honor he shared with Grant Hill, who had signed with the Detroit Pistons. The year before Kidd joined the Mavericks, they had lost 69 games and won just 13. This changed to 36 wins and 46 losses during his first years. That 23-game improvement was the largest in the NBA.

Unfortunately, after two seasons, things changed. The three leading players—including Kidd—were immature and struggled to communicate effectively. As a result, the Mavericks' performance suffered and Kidd was traded to the Phoenix Suns.

Things went better with the Suns. After a strong first season, Kidd started to hit his stride. In the 1998-99 season, he led the NBA with seven triple-doubles and had a 16.9-points-per-game career average. While with the Suns, Kidd made the All-Star Game in 1998, 2000, and 2001. He also led the NBA in assists for three years, from 1999-2001.

Kidd joined the New Jersey Nets in 2001 and immediately declared they would make the playoffs. The Nets didn't think like that—they had been in the NBA for 25 years and had been to the playoffs just seven times. Plus, the season before Kidd joined, they won just 26 games. But Kidd led by example, diving for every loose ball in the training camp and encouraging the team to show they were serious by playing preseason games to win. It worked, and the Nets became the best team in the Eastern Conference. They won 52 games that year, and didn't just reach the playoffs, but also proceeded to create some of the most memorable moments in NBA playoffs history. This included a double overtime victory against the Indiana Pacers and a comeback from a fourth-quarter collapse against the Celtics to ultimately win the series and earn a spot in the final, where they were runner-up to the Lakers. It's hard to imagine a better failure-to-success story, and it seemed to have all been from Kidd spending one training camp with the Nets.

It was the biggest improvement in the NBA that year, the 10th biggest NBA improvement ever, and the first time the Nets had ever won more than 50 games in a season. Kidd received a spot on the All-NBA First Team and narrowly missed out on the NBA MVP.

Kidd didn't get his NBA championship win until 2011, when he and the Dallas Mavericks beat the Miami Heat, but his inspiration and direction with the Nets meant he was a champion every season. Unsurprisingly, after he left the Nets, they retired his number 5 jersey.

FUN FACTS ABOUT JASON KIDD

1. Kidd now has a small ownership stake in the Nets.
2. He retired with 107 regular season triple doubles, the third-best in NBA history.
3. He was selected for 10 All-Star NBA teams and five All-NBA First Teams.
4. He is only the third player to transition from player to head coach the season after retiring. He's in good company, as the other two are Magic Johnson and Larry Bird.
5. Kidd is second in the NBA for all-time assists and steals!

QUICK TRIVIA TEST

1. When was Kidd born?

March 23, 1973.

2. When did he enter the NBA Draft?

1994.

3. What pick was he in the NBA Draft?

Second overall.

4. How many triple doubles did he have in the 1998-99 season?

Seven.

5. When did he finally win an NBA championship?

2011.

FIVE LIFE LESSONS

1. Use the lessons you learn.

You learn lessons every day of your life—the question is whether you take those lessons and learn from them or not. Kidd learned a lot about passing when he played soccer. He remembered what he had learned and found a use for it in basketball. That's part of what made him such a formidable player.

2. Inspire others.

It's one thing to be dedicated to your cause, but if you truly want success, you also need to inspire those around you. This will lift the performance of everyone involved and help you achieve any goal. That's what Kidd did when he joined the Nets.

3. Never give up.

Kidd was fiercely competitive and never gave up. That's a large part of the reason his teams always fared so well. He didn't talk a lot on court, but his consistent and continual play inspired his teammates to do their best. He led by example and effectively encouraged the entire team to never give up.

4. Believe in others.

Kidd's Nets teammate Lucious Harris once told the New York Times, "He'll never look you off. Even if you miss four shots in a row, he's still going to pass to you." That perfectly sums up Kidd's belief in his teammates and what they were capable of. More often than not, this belief was justified and rewarded. You should also believe in others and allow them to excel.

5. Change is a good thing.

Early in his career, there wasn't a faster player on the court. However, after his knee surgery in 2004, Kidd knew he would need to be a more consistent shooter. He worked with the Nets shooting coach, Bob Thate. The training worked, and he improved his shooting percentage. Change can be a good thing, so embrace it!

BONUS MATERIAL

ONE HUNDRED AFFIRMATIONS TO BUILD CONFIDENCE

Affirmations are positive statements about yourself. Repeating them daily will encourage you to believe what you're saying. This will help you to create a positive mental outlet and believe in yourself. Here are some examples:

1. My opinions are important.

2. I am worth listening to.

3. I am mentally strong.

4. I have feelings that matter.

5. I'm a good person.

6. Anything is possible if you try hard enough.

7. A positive mindset can help you achieve the impossible.

8. I face one fear every day.

9. I am who I am, and that's a good thing.

10. I love myself.

11. I'm worthy of respect.

12. I'm a good basketball player.

13. I can learn anything.

14. I'm prepared to stand up for what I believe in.

15. Everyone makes mistakes—I learn from mine.

16. I can overcome any obstacle.

17. I make good decisions.

18. I trust myself.

19. I am confident.

20. I am good at solving problems.

21. I'm a natural leader.

22. I don't follow others blindly but rather choose my own path.

23. I will succeed.

24. I trust my own instincts.

25. I focus on learning something new each day.

26. I see the positive in everyone and everything.

27. I always look for the joy in life.

28. Everyone has a good side.

29. Opportunities are everywhere, and I'm ready to seize them.

30. Every morning, I look in the mirror and smile.

31. I'm a great listener.

32. I'm curious about everything, and that's a good thing.

33. I try to make someone smile every day.

34. I'm good at helping others.

35. I'm patient with others.

36. I'm kind to others.

37. Embracing change is a good thing.

38. I don't need to fill the silence with noise.

39. I always pause to consider my actions before acting.

40. I take time to exercise daily.

41. Practicing basketball daily is important to me.

42. I am ready and able to learn something new.

43. I will persevere, no matter what the obstacles are.

44. I make friends easily.

45. I appreciate criticism as a chance to grow mentally and physically.

46. Putting my friends first is important to me.

47. Everyone is worthy in their own way.

48. Other people usually like me straight away.

49. I'm happy to share with others.

50. I play well on a team.

51. I'm proud to be part of a team.

52. I'm flexible and adaptable.

53. I listen to my elders, managers, and coaches, as they generally know what they are talking about.

54. Honesty really is the best policy.

55. Miracles do happen.

56. I know how to share my emotions and plans.

57. I choose my own boundaries.

58. I ask for help when I need to.

59. I appreciate the importance of rest and recovery.

60. I choose to eat healthily.

61. It takes five seconds of courage to achieve anything new.

62. Everyone is beautiful.

63. I'm beautiful inside and out.

64. I can tell when people are being treated unfairly.

65. I set goals for myself every day and achieve them.

66. I can build new habits when I want.

67. I behave toward others how I expect them to behave toward me.

68. I understand the importance of rest for physical and mental health.

69. I don't need other people to justify my existence.

70. I live in the present but learn from the past.

71. I can cheer myself on when needed.

72. Looking after my body is important.

73. My body is perfect the way it is.

74. I try to expand my comfort zone daily.

75. I can forgive anyone who asks.

76. I'm not afraid to apologize when I make a mistake.

77. I'm entitled to my own opinion, but respect the opinions of others.

78. Any day can become a good day.

79. I can change anything.

80. Failure is simply an opportunity to improve.

81. I love myself even when I fail.

82. Finding balance in life is important to me.

83. I am intelligent.

84. I can do it!

85. I am always a good friend.

86. I set a good example for others.

87. Money isn't the most important thing in life.

88. I choose to be happy.

89. I stand up for those in need.

90. I prefer to say nice things about people.

91. I accept everyone just the way they are.

92. I get better every day.

93. My positive energy helps others.

94. My actions make a difference.

95. I love learning new things.

96. I take care of my possessions.

97. I'm here to support loved ones whenever they need it.

98. I embrace my emotions because my feelings are valid.

99. I know my problems don't define me, it's how I react that matters.

100.   I am always in control of myself.

THE MENTAL MINDSET TO HELP YOU SUCCEED AT BASKETBALL

Most people look at basketball players and admire their physical fitness and the way they handle the ball. However, one thing that is just as important to playing well and winning is the right mental mindset. If you don't get this right, you will never learn from your failures and become the best player you can be.

Fortunately, there are several things you can do to develop a positive mental mindset.

IDENTIFY YOUR MENTAL WEAKNESS

The first step is to identify where you are mentally weak. The best approach is to pause and think about the different areas of your mindset, such as confidence, fears, your perspective, how you handle pressure or criticism, and what you do when things are going against you.

By identifying which of these areas are your weak spots, you'll be able to take steps to strengthen them.

AFFIRM YOUR POSITIVITY

With an understanding of what is limiting you, it's possible to create affirmations confirming the opposite. For example, if you fear that you'll never be a better player, create an affirmation that says you are a better player every day. This positive spin will help you change your mindset, and you'll see the difference on the court. Change all your limitations into affirmations and repeat them daily.

CREATE A MOTTO

A great follow-up to your affirmations is to create a motto. This should be based on your limitations and subsequent affirmations. You need to create a motto that you can repeat to yourself when things aren't going your way. It will bolster you mentally and help you achieve the desired result.

KEEP TRYING

You're not going to get it right every time. The secret to being a great basketball player is dedication and a commitment to trying things over and over again. That commitment will spill over onto the court, allowing you to keep going and achieve a better result than expected. All it takes is the willpower not to give up.

LEARN FROM YOUR MISTAKES

You're going to make mistakes. Missing a shot or a pass on occasion isn't a major problem. But, if you consistently make the same mistake, it is important to pause and evaluate the mistake and what's causing it. This will allow you to correct it and learn from it, making you a better player.

WELCOME CRITICISM

Criticism should always be seen as advice, no matter how harshly it is given. You can choose to get upset or to accept the criticism and use it to make you a better player. That's what the great players do. Don't forget, that people who criticize are looking at the issue from a different angle, which can help you gain a new perspective.

Creating a positive mindset will take time, but, like most things in life, if you take small steps, the positivity won't just be beneficial— it will become automatic.

YOUNG PERSONS GUIDE TO PLAYING BASKETBALL

Basketball was first invented in Massachusetts in 1891. James Naismith was a physical education instructor who came up with the sport as a less injury-prone sport than football. It was also an effective way to keep athletes training in the cold winter months.

As with most sports, the aim is to win by scoring more than the other team. In this case, to score, you need to put the ball through a basket. To start playing basketball, you'll need the following equipment and an understanding of the basic rules.

EQUIPMENT

You don't need a lot of equipment to play. You just need a basketball, a basket/net, basketball shoes, and some comfortable clothes. Having some water on hand is useful, too. Some players use knee pads, mouth guards, or protective eyewear—it typically depends if they have existing injuries.

A regulation basketball is between 9.43 inches and 9.51 inches in diameter, with a circumference of 29.5 inches and a weight of 22 ounces.

RULES OF THE GAME

To play basketball, you need a court. The size of the court depends on the age of the players. Those aged 7–8 play on a court 50 feet by 42 feet. The basket is set at eight feet high.

Players 9–11 play on a court that is 74 feet by 50 feet, with a basket that is nine feet high. Those aged 12–14 can enjoy an 84-

by-50 foot court and a basket set at 10 feet high. Anyone aged 15 and up plays on a full-sized adult court that's 94 feet by 50 feet, with a 10-foot-high basket.

All courts have a free throw line, which is where players get a free shot after they have been fouled. For younger players, it's 12 feet 10 inches from the basket, while older players shoot from 15 feet. In addition, 12- to 14-year-olds have a three-point line that is 19 feet 9 inches from the basket, while players 15 and over shoot three-pointers from 22 ft 2 inches.

The three point line is an arc set back from the basket. If you shoot and get a basket from inside this line, you get two points. If you make a basket from outside of the arc, you get three points.

The court also has baselines, which mark the ends of the court, and sidelines, which mark the sides. There is also a center circle, which is where the game starts. The ball is thrown in the air, and both team's jumpers try to reach it first and knock it to one of their players.

The aim of the game is to get the ball in the opposition's basket. However, you have to follow these rules:

- The ball can be thrown at any time using one or both hands.
- You cannot run with the ball in your hands. It must be dribbled, which means bounced against the floor as you move.
- You can use one or two hands when dribbling.
- Only your hands can touch the ball.
- You may take three steps after you stop dribbling before shooting.
- Hitting the ball with a fist is a foul.
- Three consecutive fouls give the other team a basket.
- A kids' game lasts 30 minutes, split into two 15-minute halves, with a five-minute break between them. College games have

two 20-minute halves, while NBA games have four 12-minute quarters.

PLAYERS AND POSITIONS

There are up to 12 players on a basketball team, but only five players on the court at any one time. It's a fast-paced game, so substitutions are common. The positions are:

Shooting Guard

The shooting guard is positioned on the wing and should be adept at scoring outside the three-point arc and from a long mid-range position. They need to be patient and good at finding a free position to receive a pass from the point guard. Their preferred shooting position depends on their shooting style.

Power Forward

The power forward is the player who scores the most. They need to be able to score close to the basket and from mid-range positions. Most importantly, they need to be accurate. They are usually very agile, using fancy footwork to put opponents off balance, whether attacking or defending.

Small Forward

The small forward is generally the most versatile player. They need to be aggressively attempting plays, including layups and slam dunks They also need to be good at scoring from the free throw line, as they are the most likely to be fouled. This player should be good at driving to the basket, but also at taking long-range shots.

Point Guard

The point guard is generally the shortest player on the team and the best at passing and handling the ball. Their main role is to assist the other players in scoring, although they should also be capable of creating opportunities to drop short-range shots in the net. The point guard is usually the heart of the team, creating plays.

Center

The center usually plays near the baseline, and is often the tallest player on the team. They are generally good at pulling down rebounds, contesting shots, and blocking players. In short, they are the key to a good defense.

Players need to start the game in their defined position. However, once the ball is in play, they can move anywhere.

Made in the USA
Monee, IL
26 October 2024

68703893R00069